The Sunday Horse

Contents

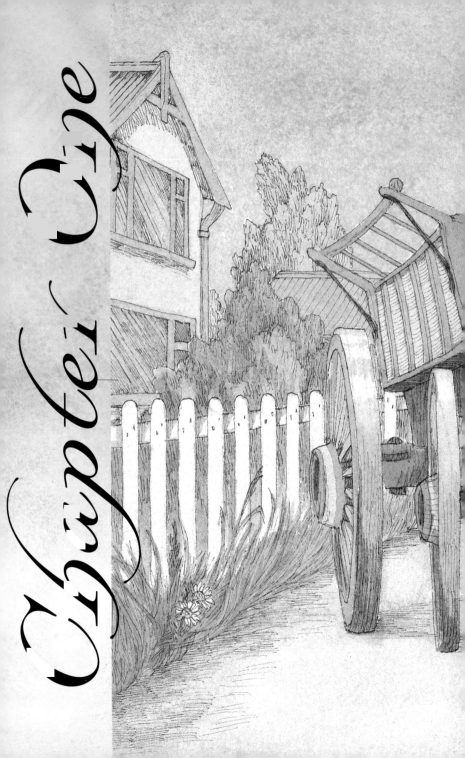

Chapter Five

The Sunday Horse

Chapter One

My name is Silvie Jenkins, and I'm going to tell you about Belle. When I woke on that rainy morning, I had no idea about what was going to happen to her. I never would have guessed how close we'd come to losing our Sundays together.

Belle is a draft horse. Her name means "beautiful," which she is. Her coat shines like polished copper. Ezra, her owner, told me he gets up early every morning to brush her. She's big, too. More like huge! I can only reach her nose to stroke it if she puts her head down to meet me first.

Early every Sunday morning during the late spring, Belle would plod down the hill past our house, pulling a big old farm wagon with seats along both sides. She would give rides at the park all day and, in the evenings, I'd see her and Ezra going back past our house on their way home.

"Giving wagon rides helps pay for your oats and chaff, doesn't it, Belle?" Ezra said the first time he stopped to let me pat her. Belle had nodded her head as if she were agreeing, and the silver rings on her harness jingled as she tossed her silky mane.

I grabbed a handful of grass. "Can I feed her?" I asked.

"Sure you can, lassie," said Ezra. "She loves her food. But watch your toes. She'd never mean to hurt you, but she could accidently step on your foot!"

I looked down at Belle's gigantic hooves and hopped back. Her hooves were bigger than my mom's biggest dinner plates.

The next Sunday, I stood at the gate with Mom, waiting for Belle. I was ready with an apple.

"You're going to spoil her," Ezra said. But he didn't mean it. He grinned, and his eyes disappeared between his sunburned cheeks and his fuzzy eyebrows. He liked it when people made a fuss over her.

I was waiting at the gate again the following week when they pulled up. I was surprised when Ezra climbed down and stood beside me. He was smaller than I had thought, and older, too. I could see the tufts of white hair sticking out from under his brown knitted hat. He leaned on his cane with hands that were thin and showed every vein.

I stared at him for a minute then looked up at Belle. How could such an old man who seemed so frail make a big animal like Belle do just what he wanted?

"Good day to you, lassie," Ezra had said (he knew my name was Silvie, but he still called me lassie). "You know Mrs. Gilly, don't you?" he continued, waving his cane toward Mrs. Gilly's house on the hill behind our house. "I want to go up and tell her my sister, Violet, says hello."

I nodded. (Poor Mrs. Gilly never had any visitors, except when my mom took her some muffins or a pie.)

"Mrs. Gilly used to go to church with my sister," explained Ezra. "But Violet doesn't get around too well these days, not like I do. So I told her I knew a lassie who would keep an eye on Belle while I took these pot pies up to the house. That's right, isn't it, Belle?"

He straightened Belle's forelock beneath her bridle before adding, "You'll watch out for Belle for me, won't you?"

I nodded. "Yes." But my heart thumped. "What if something goes wrong? What if she tries to run off? What if a car comes racing around the corner and scares her?"

"Don't you worry," he said, reaching up and patting Belle's neck. "Cars don't scare our Belle."

Chapter Two

Chapter Two

So a minute later I was standing there, holding Belle's reins while Ezra lifted a bag down from the cart. I watched him hobble across the sidewalk with it and go in through Mrs. Gilly's gate.

Suddenly I felt a jerk on the reins. I looked around. Belle was tossing her head, and her harness was jingling. She was rolling her eyes. What would she do next?

Then I remembered the apple I had in my pocket. She could smell it, and she wanted it. Keeping my hand flat and my fingers out of the way, I held the apple up as high as I could. Belle chomped it in half with her large yellow teeth. The other half fell to the ground. The juice went everywhere. It ran down my arm and into my sleeve.

"Belle! You're a mess!" I said. But she kept on munching until she was done. Then she waited while I rescued the other half off the ground.

When that was all gone, she looked around for more. She nosed at my pocket – almost pushing me over – but I didn't have anything else. I began to panic about what to do next.

Then I saw the grass growing from under our fence. If I held the reins by the very end, I could almost reach it. The wagon creaked, and Belle's hooves crunched on the gravel as she moved over to help me. By the time Ezra got back, we'd cleaned up all the grass on our side of the road. I only wished someone had seen us.

"Thank you, lassie," Ezra said, climbing on the wagon. "Was she a good girl?"

"Great!" I said.

"Next Sunday you can come to the park with Belle if your folks say it's OK. We could use a good helper."

He flicked the reins, and Belle leaned into her harness. The wagon rolled out onto the road, and I watched them all the way to the next corner. I was bursting with pride. I had looked after Belle by myself with no one keeping an eye on me! And next Sunday I'd be going to the park. Jason and Bradley, two of the boys from school, often went there. They'd been boasting about having rides in Belle's wagon. They hadn't believed me when I told them I was Belle's friend. Now I'd show them!

I raced inside. My parents were having breakfast. Mom was making toast, and Dad was pouring coffee.

"Have you been out there talking to the horse?" Dad said.

"Yes! And Ezra said next Sunday I can ride with him down to the park if you and Mom say it's OK. I'm going to be Belle's helper."

Dad frowned. "Who is this Ezra person, anyway?"

"Mrs. Gilly has known him for a long time. He's been very kind to her, and I've met him, too," said Mom.

"Well," said Dad, "if Mom says it's OK, then I suppose it'll be all right. But we might come down to the park to see how things are going."

Chapter Three

Chapter Three

All that week at school, I kept bragging to Bradley and Jason about how I'd be going to the park with Belle and Ezra. I told them how Ezra had left me in charge of Belle.

"Don't be silly!" Jason said. "Who'd let you look after a horse like Belle?"

"You'll see!" I said. "Just make sure you're at the park on Sunday!"

On Saturday night, I was so worried, I couldn't sleep. What if it rained and Ezra decided not to go? What if I slept in and he went right past our house without stopping? What if he just changed his mind?

But it didn't rain, and when Ezra said, "Whoa, Belle," I was waiting at our gate. I scrambled up on the wagon and sat on the nearest seat.

"You can't drive Belle from way back there," said Ezra. "Come and sit up front!"

Driving Belle was better than I had ever imagined. The best part was when we went into the park and I had ahold of the reins. Ezra had ahold of them, too, but Bradley and Jason couldn't see that. They watched us with their eyes opened so wide, that I thought their eyeballs would pop out. I couldn't stop giggling.

"You can collect the money," Ezra said. I buckled the leather bag around my waist. The rides were a dollar each, so giving the right change wasn't hard.

We had hot dogs for lunch. Ezra bought them at the stall. Belle had her lunch out of a bag that Ezra hung around her neck. Now and then, she blew into it, puffing chaff into the air.

Dad came down to the park after lunch. First he waved to Ezra and me from the rose gardens and came over for a chat. Then I saw him by the pine trees, where Belle set down her passengers and took on new ones. He was "keeping an eye on me" like he said he would.

I think he left about mid-afternoon, because I didn't see him after that.

Just before sunset, we began the journey home. The wagon rocked from side to side, and the wheels rumbled rhythmically. I almost went to sleep.

"Here we are. Home again," Ezra said as the wagon stopped with a jolt.

My eyes opened, and I climbed down unsteadily from the wagon.

"Bye," I said. "And thanks."

I watched Ezra shake the reins to tell Belle to walk on. He turned and waved. "See you next Sunday?"

I nodded and waved back. It had been fun, especially seeing the faces of Bradley and Jason, but I was tired. My legs were so stiff from climbing in and out of the wagon, I thought maybe one day was more than enough.

Chapter Four

Chapter Four

My school had a field day the following Saturday afternoon, so I didn't have time to think about going to the park with Belle. And on Saturday night it rained. It rained and rained! It thumped down on the roof and ran through the gutters in rivers.

It had stopped when I woke up on Sunday morning, but the sky was gray. I didn't want to get out of bed.

Ezra won't take Belle to the park today, I told myself. I hugged the blankets up under my chin and shut my eyes. But I was wrong, because soon I heard the clip-clop of Belle's hooves. I pulled the blankets up higher. If I wasn't at the gate, Ezra would drive on. He'd guess I wouldn't be going to the park on a day like this.

Then I heard him. "Whoa, Belle," he said. The wagon had stopped. Belle would be expecting me. I'd never missed having a treat for her since that first Sunday. If I hid an apple in my pocket, she'd push with her nose until she found it. She'd be looking toward the gate, her ears moving to catch the sound of my running feet.

I pushed the blankets back and got to my knees to look out the window. Yes. There she was. The chilly wind ruffled her mane. She shook her head. But where was Ezra? He wasn't sitting up on the wagon. His seat was empty. He must have gone to see Mrs. Gilly. Belle was there alone.

"I'd better go out," I muttered. I pulled my sweater and jeans on over my pajamas and felt under the bed for my sneakers.

If I took long enough, Ezra would be back and I wouldn't have to go out in the cold. But when I looked out again, Belle was still alone. I put some sugar cubes in my pocket and opened the door. Belle was stamping her feet. She was tired of waiting.

As I reached the gate, she leaned into her harness and dragged the wagon across the road. She was after the long grass growing on the far side. She'd waited for the treat I always brought and, when it didn't come, she'd decided to get some grass for herself.

There were no houses on the other side of the road. Just grass and a steep bank down into a gully. A row of pine trees grew near the bottom. Beyond that there was a little stream that disappeared into a trickling drain.

Ezra had seen Belle walking away from where he stood on Mrs. Gilly's porch. "Whoa, Belle! Whoa!" he shouted, almost running down Mrs. Gilly's sidewalk. But Belle had expected food, and she was going to get some. She leaned over to reach the grass.

The clay that formed the edge of the road was soft after the rain. It gave way under the wheels of the heavy wagon. The weight of the wagon pushed forward onto Belle.

Belle took a step down the bank to get out of its way, but the wagon pushed her farther down the bank, and even her great strength couldn't hold it back. A moment later, she was sliding down the bank, toward the trees, trying to dig in with her huge hooves all the way.

Chapter Five

Chapter Five

I rushed over and saw that Belle had tried to take the wagon through a gap between the trees. I'd heard the crash as the wagon tipped over and landed on its side. Belle was lying on her side, snorting and whinnying and scraping the ground with her hooves.

"Belle! Belle!" cried Ezra, slithering down the bank, trying in vain to steady himself with his cane.

I stayed up on the road. I couldn't go down. I didn't want to see Belle. She was hurt and it was my fault. I should have been there taking care of her.

Ezra knelt beside her and stroked her head. "It's all right, girl," he said. "I'll get you out of here. Don't you worry. I'm here. Everything is going to be OK."

As long as Ezra stayed there talking to Belle, she lay still, but when he stood up to reach the buckles on her harness, she began to struggle again.

Ezra looked up toward the road. "Can someone come down and help?" he called.

I looked around. The crash had brought people out of their houses. They were lined up along the bank.

"I want someone she knows," Ezra said. "Someone to talk to her."

Someone she knows? That had to be me. There wasn't anyone else. I half-climbed, half-slid down the bank and crouched beside Belle.

"Is she hurt? Is she going to be all right, Ezra?"

"We'll have to see," said Ezra. "But right now she's scared. Talk to her and pet her, the way you always do."

She's scared, I thought. But what about me? It was one thing feeding her apples and making a fuss over her outside my gate. It would be quite different, though, trying to calm this huge frightened animal! But what else could I do?

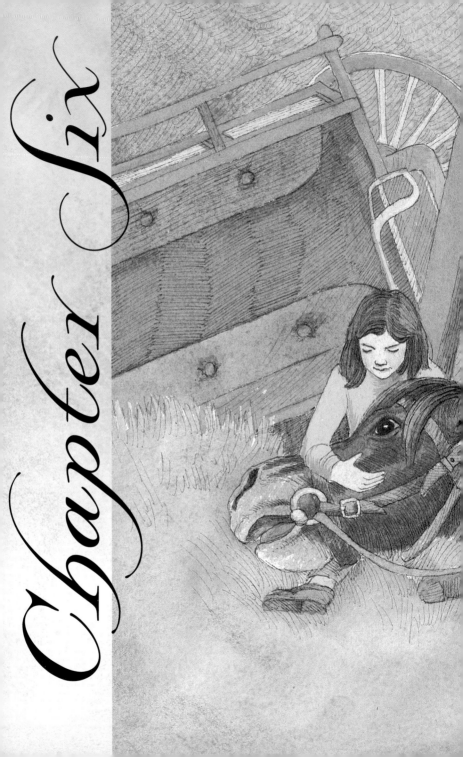

Chapter Six

Chapter Six

I crouched down beside Belle and stroked her neck. "Hello, Belle," I said softly. She stopped rolling her eyes and lifted her head to look at me. I felt less afraid. "Good girl," I told her. "Lie still while Ezra loosens your harness."

I sat down on the damp grass. Belle put her head on my lap. It was so heavy, I couldn't move. I went on patting her and talking to her for ages while Ezra struggled with the buckles and straps of the harness. My legs were stiff and my back hurt. Rain dripped from the trees, and a cold wind blew up the gully.

At last, I felt Ezra's hand on my shoulder. "All right now, lassie," he said. "You've done well. Stand back and we'll see if she can get up."

He held Belle's head while I wriggled out from underneath it.

"She's not badly hurt, is she?" I wasn't frightened of her anymore. But I was frightened *for* her.

I stood back and watched while Ezra gave the reins a tug. "Come on, Belle," he said. "Up!"

Belle lifted her head. Then she pushed herself up on her front legs. Finally she gave a mighty heave and she was standing.

She set her legs apart and shook herself. Dirt and squashed grass flew into the air, and I heard the sound of clapping from the road.

"Come on, Belle," said Ezra. He gave the reins a gentle pull and steered her along the little stream and up a path that led to the road above.

Chapter Seven

Chapter Seven

A truck came that afternoon with a crane to lift the wagon out of the gully. But Ezra was not with it, so I couldn't find out how Belle was.

"If he walked Belle home, there can't be too much wrong with her," Dad said at lunchtime. He was getting sick of my long face.

"But I don't even know where she lives," I argued. "And I didn't get a chance to say good-bye."

I spent the afternoon staring out my bedroom window, remembering how Belle pulled up at the gate every Sunday and waited for me.

Maybe Ezra won't be able to take her to the park anymore, I thought. I'll never see my Sunday Horse again. Could this have been Belle's last Sunday?

"I went over to see Mrs. Gilly," Dad said later on. "She told me where Ezra lives. If you're still worried about Belle, we'll take you to see her."

I was the first one to the car, my pockets bulging with treats. The trip to Ezra's place seemed to take forever.

At last we came to a tiny farm cottage. It had a plain fence across the front and apple trees on each side of the driveway. Mom and Dad walked behind me as I ran at breakneck speed up the path.

"You're here to see your friend," Ezra said with a smile.

"Is she all right?" I asked.

He nodded. "She's fine now."

Belle was grazing in a paddock behind the house. When she heard the gate, she lifted her head and came to meet us.

I held up an apple and she took a big bite. The juice went everywhere. It ran down my arm and into my sleeve – like the first time I gave her an apple.

"It was my fault she got hurt," I said. "If I'd been out there, she wouldn't have tried to get the grass."

"No. It was my fault," Ezra said. "I shouldn't have left her alone. I always knew that she couldn't be trusted where food was concerned. But it won't happen again."

"Do you mean this is her last Sunday?" I asked. "Won't she be giving any more rides at the park?"

"Not until her old wagon is fixed," Ezra said. He waved his hand toward the wagon. "But we'll be back, lassie. You can't keep old warhorses like Belle and me down."

Something nudged at my shoulder. It was Belle. She blew gently in my face. I'd forgotten the sugar cubes I'd put in my pocket that morning, but she knew they were there. She's so smart. I'm really proud to have Belle the Sunday Horse for my friend.

From the Author

Although I write fiction, most of my stories have something in them that is true. I really did know a horse that slid down a bank, just the way Belle did. But the horse I knew was not a park horse; she was a milk-cart horse. Every morning, she delivered milk to the houses where I lived. She was trained to walk down the middle of the road while the driver ran back and forth with milk and empty bottles. But, like Silvie from the story, the driver didn't think about the tasty grass that grew alongside the road. I'm sure, however, you'll be pleased to hear that my cart horse was rescued safely, too.

Marie Gibson

From the Illustrator

I live on a farm in the west of England. It's the same farm where I was born. We have cows and pigs, and we grow wheat. My neighbor has a Clydesdale horse called Jemima, and I used photos and drawings of Jemima for the pictures of Belle, the Sunday Horse. I spend a lot of time working on book illustrations, and I especially like to draw animals, birds, and flowers.

John Hurford

Written by **Marie Gibson**
Illustrated by **John Hurford**
Edited by **Sue Ledington**
Designed by **Nicola Evans**

© 1997 Shortland Publications Limited
All rights reserved.

02 01 00 99 98 97
10 9 8 7 6 5 4 3 2 1

Distributed in the United States by
   Rigby
   a division of Reed Elsevier Inc.
   P.O. Box 797
   Crystal Lake, IL 60039-0797

Printed by Colorcraft, Hong Kong
ISBN: 0-7901-1802-5